To:

_____

From:

_____

So This Is
How Being a
Grandmother
Feels

Chris Shea

Andrews McMeel
Publishing

Kansas City · Sydney · London

So This Is
How Being a
Grandmother
Feels

Grandbabies...

Who instructs

these

tiny

thieves

to

steal our

hearts

and

take our breath

away?

And why

isn't it

written

anywhere

that the

first gift

we'll give

to our

grandchildren

won't be

a ducky

or a

blanket

or a new pair

of jammies.

The first gift

we

give

is our

heart.

So this

is

how being

a grandmother

feels...

like the

sun coming out

for the

very first

time

and the

grass growing

greener

on

your side of the

fence

and the sky

looking bluer

than

ever before,

because

Heaven's

come closer

to

earth.

How

could we ever

prepare

ourselves

for that moment

we long await

and plan for

and dream

of,

.

because

there's no way

of knowing

how wonderful

walking on air

is going to feel.

Becoming a

grandmother

changes our

thinking.

And what

seemed like enough

long ago for our children

simply

will no longer do.

So two pairs

of sleepers

turns into six pairs

and

ten flannel blankets

are

better than three

were,

one

little teddy bear

isn't enough,

and a

night light

that throws stars

on the

nursery ceiling—

that's not a luxury, really.

We're blessed

that

we're seeing

our children

as

parents,

raising

their families

with wisdom

and

love

and filling

our hearts

with

pride.

So

this

is what

being

a grandmother

is.

It's

feeling

the need

to remind

the new

mothers

to cherish

the things

they think

they won't miss,

like

tiny little fingerprints

all over

the

glass;

and it's wanting

to whisper

to all the

new fathers

that

an unmowed lawn

will

always

wait.

But

childhood

hurries by.

This

is what

every grandmother

knows:

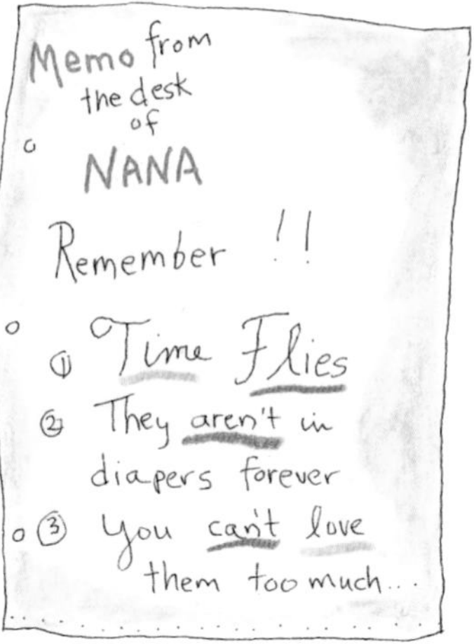
Memo from the desk of NANA
Remember !!
① Time Flies
② They aren't in diapers forever
③ You can't love them too much...

that

granddaughters

are

poems

with

heartbeats,

that

grandsons

are

godsends

from

heaven,

and that no matter

how many,

no matter

how

old,

grandchildren

continue to

take us

to places

our hearts

never

knew

were there.

Andrews McMeel Publishing, LLC
an Andrews McMeel Universal company
1130 Walnut Street, Kansas City, Missouri 64106

www.andrewsmcmeel.com

14 15 16 17 18 TEN 10 9 8 7 6 5 4 3 2 1

ISBN: 978-1-4494-5103-5

Library of Congress Catalog Card Number: 2014934528

ATTENTION: SCHOOLS AND BUSINESSES

Andrews McMeel books are available at quantity discounts with
bulk purchase for educational, business, or sales promotional use.
For information, please e-mail the Andrews McMeel Publishing
Special Sales Department: specialsales@amuniversal.com